Allegro Barbaro

and Other Short Works
for Solo Piano

BÉLA BARTÓK

DOVER PUBLICATIONS, INC.
Mineola, New York

Bibliographical Note

This Dover edition, first published in 1998, is a new compilation of works by Béla Bartók originally published separately by Universal Edition. *Allegro barbaro, Romanian Folk Dances, Romanian Christmas Carols* and *Suite, Op. 14,* were originally published in 1918; *Fifteen Hungarian Peasant Songs* and *Etudes, Op. 18,* in 1920; *Improvisations on Hungarian Peasant Tunes, Op. 20,* in 1922.

The Dover edition adds a unified list of contents and new headings throughout. Bartók's "alternate versions for concert performance" of selected Christmas Carols or parts of Carols were originally grouped as an appendix at the end of the work. To facilitate their use, the Dover edition interleaves complete concert alternatives in their appropriate numerical sequence in the score itself; alternate phrases have been inserted in the music as small-note *ossias* where they occur.

We are indebted to Barbara Bollok, President of Molnár Travel Agency, New York City, and George Mendel of *Time* magazine—translators for the Hungarian Consulate, New York—for their kind assistance in verifying spellings and English translations of the original Hungarian and Romanian titles.

International Standard Book Number: 0-486-40110-3

Manufactured in the United States of America
Dover Publications, Inc., 31 East 2nd Street, Mineola, N.Y. 11501

Contents

Allegro Barbaro

and Other Short Works
for Solo Piano

Allegro barbaro

(1911)

Tempo giusto. ($\stackrel{\downarrow}{=}$ 76 – 84)

2

Romanian Folk Dances

Román népi táncok (1915)

I. Stick game • *Joc cu bâta*

II. Peasant costume · *Braul*

(la 2.volta: poco ritard.)

(25″)

III. Standing still · *Pe loc*

IV. Song of the mountain horn
Buciumeana

V. A garden gate in Romania
V Poarca Românească

VI. Little one · *Maruntel*

Ossia:

(86⁷)

Romanian
Christmas Carols

Román Karácsonyi dallamok **(1915)**

First Series

(29'')

2. Allegro. (♩. = 126.)

3. Allegro. (♩ = 130.)
marcatissimo

(13″)

marcato

marcatissimo

*) ⌐_⌐ = Pedalbezeichnung.

(26″)

3. [Concert version]

5. [Concert version]

6. Andante. (♩ = 88.)

p dolce

p dolce

cresc.

poco rit.

sopra

mf

(29″)

8. [Including a concert *ossia*, mm. 17–22]

Allegretto. (♩ = 126.)

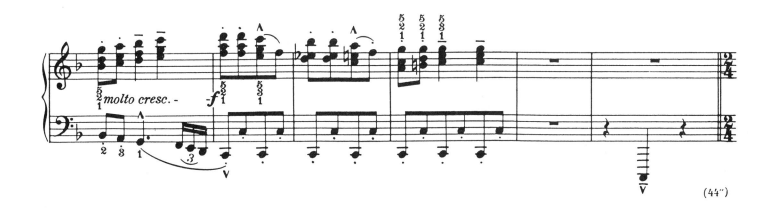

(44")

9. Allegro. (♩ = 160.)

(19")

10. Più allegro. ($\bullet$ = 168.)

sempre *f*

(15″)

Second Series

1. Molto moderato. ($\bullet$ = 84.)

f pesante

(34")

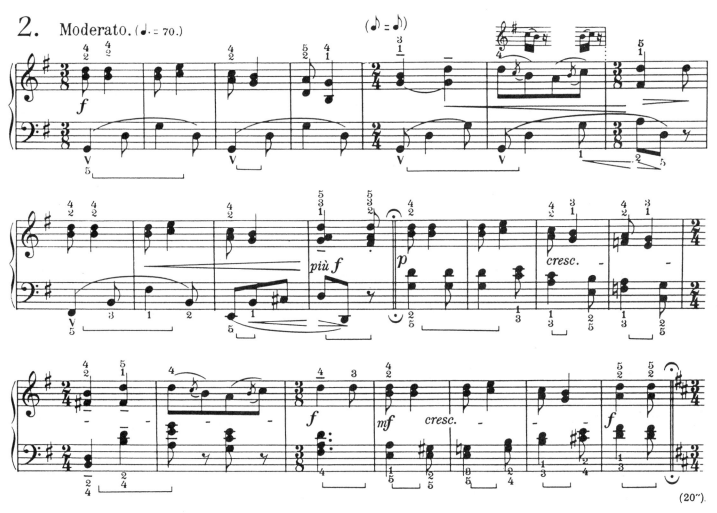

(20")

4. [Including a concert *ossia*, mm. 13–18]

5.

Moderato. ($\downarrow$ = 112-104.)

$(35'')$

5. [Concert version]

6. **Andante.** ($\quad$ = 84 – 80.)

7. Variante della precedente.

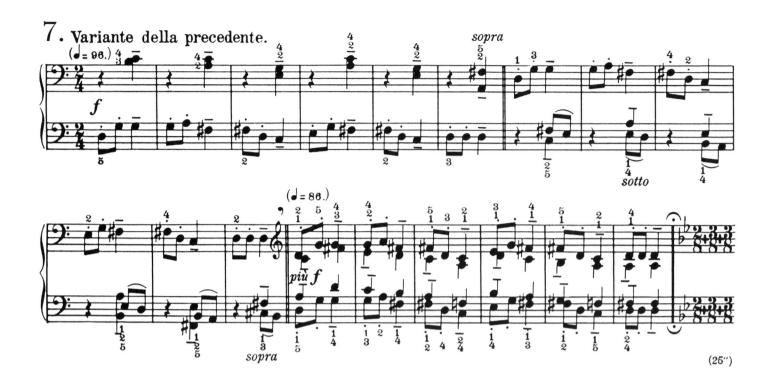

(25″)

7. [Concert version]

6. [Reprise]

8. Allegro. (♩ = 108.)

(34″)

8. [Concert version]

9. [Including a concert *ossia,* mm. 6–end]

Allegretto. (♩ = 108.)

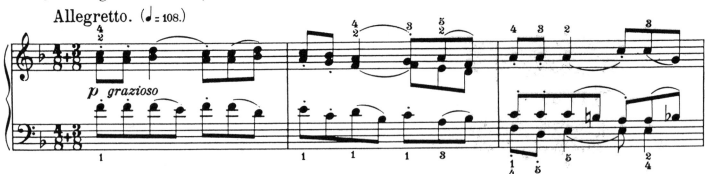

[concert *ossia* continued below]

(25″)

10. [Including a concert *ossia*, mm. 1–6]

Allegro. (♩ = 140.)

Fifteen
Hungarian Peasant Songs

Tizenöt magyar paraszt'dal (1914–18)

Four Old Tunes

Ballade
Theme with variations

Old Dance Tunes

Suite

Op. 14 (1918)

1.

Durée d'exécution ca 2'

2.

*) ⌐___⌐ = Pedalbezeichnung.

Tranquillo. (♩.= 92)

Tempo I.

Durée d'exécution ca 1'50"

3.

4.

Etudes

Op. 18 (1920)

I.

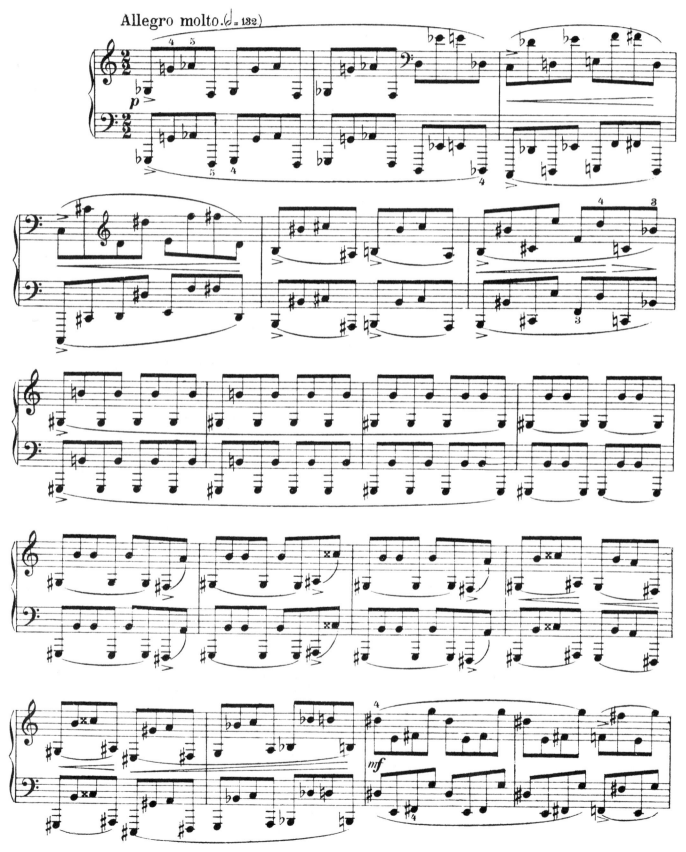

II.

Andante sostenuto. (♩=86-92)

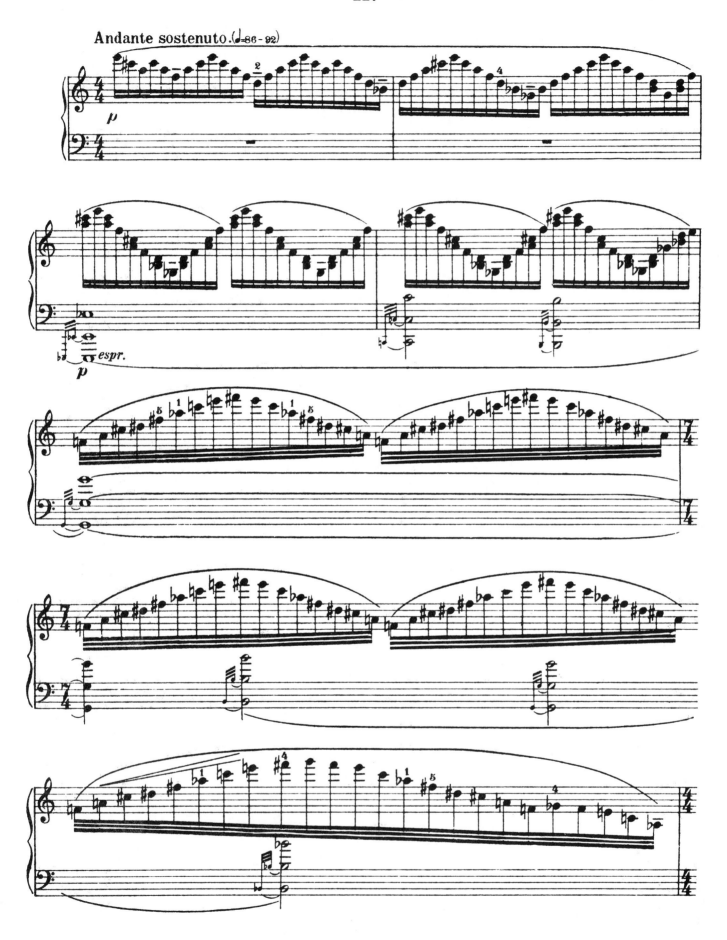

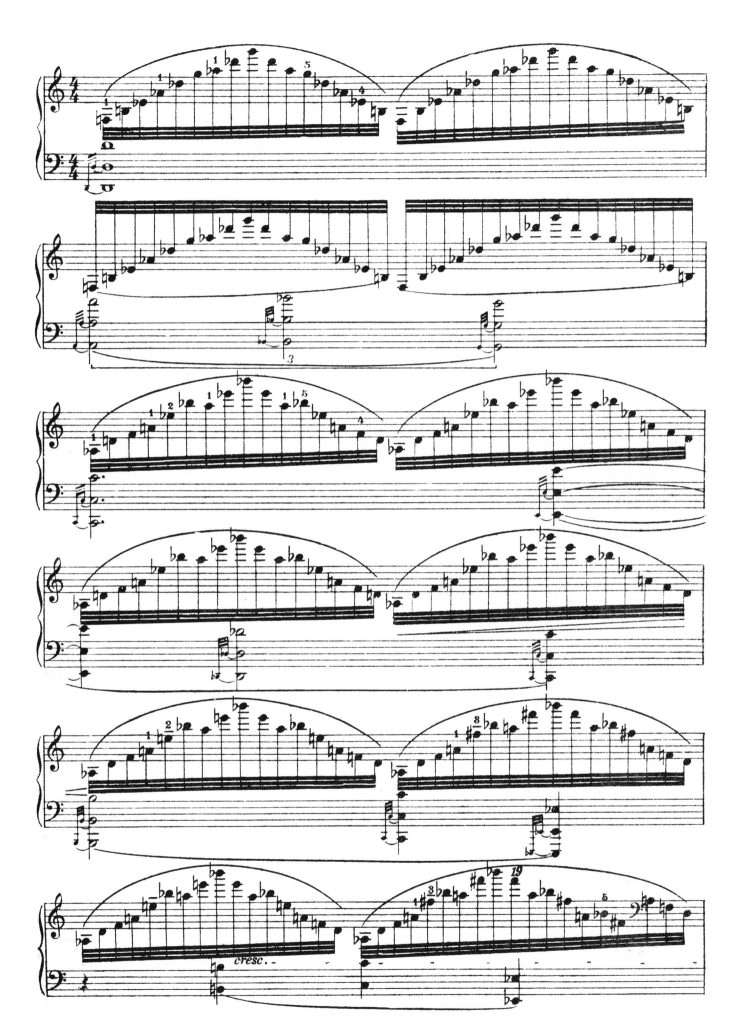

III.

Improvisations
on Hungarian Peasant Songs

Improvizaciok Magyar Nepdalra

Op. 20 (1920)

I.

II.

III.

IV.

V.

VI.

VIII.

END OF EDITION

Dover Piano and Keyboard Editions

THE WELL-TEMPERED CLAVIER: Books I and II, Complete, Johann Sebastian Bach. All 48 preludes and fugues in all major and minor keys. Authoritative Bach-Gesellschaft edition. Explanation of ornaments in English, tempo indications, music corrections. 208pp. 9⅜ × 12¼. 24532-2 Pa. **$9.95**

KEYBOARD MUSIC, J. S. Bach. Bach-Gesellschaft edition. For harpsichord, piano, other keyboard instruments. English Suites, French Suites, Six Partitas, Goldberg Variations, Two-Part Inventions, Three-Part Sinfonias. 312pp. 8⅛ × 11. 22360-4 Pa. **$11.95**

ITALIAN CONCERTO, CHROMATIC FANTASIA AND FUGUE AND OTHER WORKS FOR KEYBOARD, Johann Sebastian Bach. Sixteen of Bach's best-known, most-performed and most-recorded works for the keyboard, reproduced from the authoritative Bach-Gesellschaft edition. 112pp. 9 × 12. 25387-2 Pa. **$8.95**

COMPLETE KEYBOARD TRANSCRIPTIONS OF CONCERTOS BY BAROQUE COMPOSERS, Johann Sebastian Bach. Sixteen concertos by Vivaldi, Telemann and others, transcribed for solo keyboard instruments. Bach-Gesellschaft edition. 128pp. 9⅜ × 12¼. 25529-8 Pa. **$9.95**

ORGAN MUSIC, J. S. Bach. Bach-Gesellschaft edition. 93 works. 6 Trio Sonatas, German Organ Mass, Orgelbüchlein, Six Schubler Chorales, 18 Choral Preludes. 357pp. 8⅛ × 11. 22359-0 Pa. **$13.95**

COMPLETE PRELUDES AND FUGUES FOR ORGAN, Johann Sebastian Bach. All 25 of Bach's complete sets of preludes and fugues (i.e. compositions written as pairs), from the authoritative Bach-Gesellschaft edition. 168pp. 8⅜ × 11. 24816-X Pa. **$10.95**

TOCCATAS, FANTASIAS, PASSACAGLIA AND OTHER WORKS FOR ORGAN, J. S. Bach. Over 20 best-loved works including Toccata and Fugue in D minor, BWV 565; Passacaglia and Fugue in C minor, BWV 582, many more. Bach-Gesellschaft edition. 176pp. 9 × 12. 25403-8 Pa. **$10.95**

TWO- AND THREE-PART INVENTIONS, J. S. Bach. Reproduction of original autograph ms. Edited by Eric Simon. 62pp. 8⅛ × 11. 21982-8 Pa. **$8.95**

THE 36 FANTASIAS FOR KEYBOARD, Georg Philipp Telemann. Graceful compositions by 18th-century master. 1923 Breslauer edition. 80pp. 8⅛ × 11. 25365-1 Pa. **$6.95**

GREAT KEYBOARD SONATAS, Carl Philipp Emanuel Bach. Comprehensive two-volume edition contains 51 sonatas by second, most important son of Johann Sebastian Bach. Originality, rich harmony, delicate workmanship. Authoritative French edition. Total of 384pp. 8⅜ × 11¼. Series I 24853-4 Pa. **$9.95**
Series II 24854-2 Pa. **$10.95**

KEYBOARD WORKS/Series One: Ordres I-XIII; Series Two: Ordres XIV-XXVII and Miscellaneous Pieces, François Couperin. Over 200 pieces. Reproduced directly from edition prepared by Johannes Brahms and Friedrich Chrysander. Total of 496pp. 8⅛ × 11.
Series I 25795-9 Pa. **$10.95**
Series II 25796-7 Pa. **$11.95**

KEYBOARD WORKS FOR SOLO INSTRUMENTS, G. F. Handel. 35 neglected works from Handel's vast oeuvre, originally jotted down as improvisations. Includes Eight Great Suites, others. New sequence. 174pp. 9⅜ × 12¼. 24338-9 Pa. **$10.95**

WORKS FOR ORGAN AND KEYBOARD, Jan Pieterszoon Sweelinck. Nearly all of early Dutch composer's difficult-to-find keyboard works. Chorale variations; toccatas, fantasias; variations on secular, dance tunes. Also, incomplete and/or modified works, plus fantasia by John Bull. 272pp. 9 × 12. 24935-2 Pa. **$12.95**

ORGAN WORKS, Dietrich Buxtehude. Complete organ works of extremely influential pre-Bach composer. Toccatas, preludes, chorales, more. Definitive Breitkopf & Härtel edition. 320pp. 8⅜ × 11¼. (Available in U.S. only) 25682-0 Pa. **$14.95**

THE FUGUES ON THE MAGNIFICAT FOR ORGAN OR KEYBOARD, Johann Pachelbel. 94 pieces representative of Pachelbel's magnificent contribution to keyboard composition; can be played on the organ, harpsichord or piano. 100pp. 9 × 12. (Available in U.S. only) 25037-7 Pa. **$8.95**

MY LADY NEVELLS BOOKE OF VIRGINAL MUSIC, William Byrd. 42 compositions in modern notation from 1591 ms. For any keyboard instrument. 245pp. 8⅛ × 11. 22246-2 Pa. **$13.95**

ELIZABETH ROGERS HIR VIRGINALL BOOKE, edited with calligraphy by Charles J. F. Cofone. All 112 pieces from noted 1656 manuscript, most never before published. Composers include Thomas Brewer, William Byrd, Orlando Gibbons, etc. 125pp. 9 × 12. 23138-0 Pa. **$10.95**

THE FITZWILLIAM VIRGINAL BOOK, edited by J. Fuller Maitland, W. B. Squire. Famous early 17th-century collection of keyboard music, 300 works by Morley, Byrd, Bull, Gibbons, etc. Modern notation. Total of 938pp. 8⅜ × 11. Two-vol. set. 21068-5, 21069-3 Pa. **$34.90**

GREAT KEYBOARD SONATAS, Series I and Series II, Domenico Scarlatti. 78 of the most popular sonatas reproduced from the G. Ricordi edition edited by Alessandro Longo. Total of 320pp. 8⅛ × 11¼.
Series I 24996-4 Pa. **$9.95**
Series II 25003-2 Pa. **$9.95**

COMPLETE PIANO SONATAS, Joseph Haydn. 52 sonatas reprinted from authoritative Breitkopf & Härtel edition. Extremely clear and readable; ample space for notes, analysis. 464pp. 9⅜ × 12¼.
24726-0 Pa. **$11.95**
24727-9 Pa. **$11.95**

BAGATELLES, RONDOS AND OTHER SHORTER WORKS FOR PIANO, Ludwig van Beethoven. Most popular and most performed shorter works, including Rondo a capriccio in G and Andante in F. Breitkopf & Härtel edition. 128pp. 9⅜ × 12¼. 25392-9 Pa. **$8.95**

COMPLETE VARIATIONS FOR SOLO PIANO, Ludwig van Beethoven. Contains all 21 sets of Beethoven's piano variations, including the extremely popular *Diabelli Variations, Op. 120.* 240pp. 9⅜ × 12¼. 25188-8 Pa. **$12.95**

COMPLETE PIANO SONATAS, Ludwig van Beethoven. All sonatas in fine Schenker edition, with fingering, analytical material. One of best modern editions. 615pp. 9 × 12. Two-vol. set. 23134-8, 23135-6 Pa. **$25.90**

COMPLETE SONATAS FOR PIANOFORTE SOLO, Franz Schubert. All 15 sonatas. Breitkopf and Härtel edition. 293pp. 9⅜ × 12¼. 22647-6 Pa. **$13.95**

DANCES FOR SOLO PIANO, Franz Schubert. Over 350 waltzes, minuets, landler, ecossaises, other charming, melodic dance compositions reprinted from the authoritative Breitkopf & Härtel edition. 192pp. 9⅜ × 12¼. 26107-7 Pa. **$11.95**

*Available from your music dealer or write for **free** Music Catalog to Dover Publications, Inc., Dept. MUBI, 31 East 2nd Street, Mineola, N.Y. 11501.*

Dover Piano and Keyboard Editions

ORGAN WORKS, César Franck. Composer's best-known works for organ, including Six Pieces, Trois Pieces, and Trois Chorals. Oblong format for easy use at keyboard. Authoritative Durand edition. 208pp. 11⅜ × 8¼. 25517-4 Pa. **$13.95**

IBERIA AND ESPAÑA: Two Complete Works for Solo Piano, Isaac Albeniz. Spanish composer's greatest piano works in authoritative editions. Includes the popular "Tango". 192pp. 9 × 12. 25367-8 Pa. **$10.95**

GOYESCAS, SPANISH DANCES AND OTHER WORKS FOR SOLO PIANO, Enrique Granados. Great Spanish composer's most admired, most performed suites for the piano, in definitive Spanish editions. 176pp. 9 × 12. 25481-X Pa. **$9.95**

SELECTED PIANO COMPOSITIONS, César Franck, edited by Vincent d'Indy. Outstanding selection of influential French composer's piano works, including early pieces and the two masterpieces—Prelude, Choral and Fugue; and Prelude, Aria and Finale. Ten works in all. 138pp. 9 × 12. 23269-7 Pa. **$10.95**

THE COMPLETE PRELUDES AND ETUDES FOR PIANOFORTE SOLO, Alexander Scriabin. All the preludes and études including many perfectly spun miniatures. Edited by K. N. Igumnov and Y. I. Mil'shteyn. 250pp. 9 × 12. 22919-X Pa. **$11.95**

COMPLETE PIANO SONATAS, Alexander Scriabin. All ten of Scriabin's sonatas, reprinted from an authoritative early Russian edition. 256pp. 8⅜ × 11¼. 25850-5 Pa. **$12.95**

COMPLETE PRELUDES AND ETUDES-TABLEAUX, Serge Rachmaninoff. Forty-one of his greatest works for solo piano, including the riveting C minor, G-minor and B-minor preludes, in authoritative editions. 208pp. 8⅜ × 11¼.
25696-0 Pa. **$11.95**

COMPLETE PIANO SONATAS, Sergei Prokofiev. Definitive Russian edition of nine sonatas (1907–1953), among the most important compositions in the modern piano repertoire. 288pp. 8⅜ × 11¼. (Available in U.S. only) 25689-8 Pa. **$12.95**

GYMNOPÉDIES, GNOSSIENNES AND OTHER WORKS FOR PIANO, Erik Satie. The largest Satie collection of piano works yet published, 17 in all, reprinted from the original French editions. 176pp. 9 × 12. (Not available in France or Germany) 25978-1 Pa. **$10.95**

TWENTY SHORT PIECES FOR PIANO (Sports et Divertissements), Erik Satie. French master's brilliant thumbnail sketches—verbal and musical—of various outdoor sports and amusements. English translations, 20 illustrations. Rare, limited 1925 edition. 48pp. 12 × 8⅞. (Not available in France or Germany) 24365-6 Pa. **$6.95**

COMPLETE PRELUDES, IMPROMPTUS AND VALSES-CAPRICES, Gabriel Fauré. Eighteen elegantly wrought piano works in authoritative editions. Only one-volume collection. 144pp. 9 × 12. (Not available in France or Germany) 25789-4 Pa. **$8.95**

PIANO MUSIC OF BÉLA BARTÓK, Series I, Béla Bartók. New, definitive Archive Edition incorporating composer's corrections. Includes *Funeral March* from *Kossuth*, *Fourteen Bagatelles*, Bartók's break to modernism. 167pp. 9 × 12. (Available in U.S. only) 24108-4 Pa. **$11.95**

PIANO MUSIC OF BÉLA BARTÓK, Series II, Béla Bartók. Second in the Archie Edition incorporating composer's corrections. 85 short pieces *For Children*, *Two Elegies*, *Two Rumanian Dances*, etc. 192pp. 9 × 12. (Available in U.S. only) 24109-2 Pa. **$11.95**

FRENCH PIANO MUSIC, AN ANTHOLOGY, Isidor Phillipp (ed.). 44 complete works, 1670–1905, by Lully, Couperin, Rameau, Alkan, Saint-Saëns, Delibes, Bizet, Godard, many others; favorites, lesser-known examples, but all top quality. 188pp. 9 × 12. (Not available in France or Germany) 23381-2 Pa. **$9.95**

NINETEENTH-CENTURY EUROPEAN PIANO MUSIC: Unfamiliar Masterworks, John Gillespie (ed.). Difficult-to-find études, toccatas, polkas, impromptus, waltzes, etc., by Albéniz, Bizet, Chabrier, Fauré, Smetana, Richard Strauss, Wagner and 16 other composers. 62 pieces. 343pp. 9 × 12. (Not available in France or Germany) 23447-9 Pa. **$19.95**

RARE MASTERPIECES OF RUSSIAN PIANO MUSIC: Eleven Pieces by Glinka, Balakirev, Glazunov and Others, edited by Dmitry Feofanov. Glinka's *Prayer*, Balakirev's *Reverie*, Liapunov's *Transcendental Etude, Op. 11, No. 10*, and eight others—full, authoritative scores from Russian texts. 144pp. 9 × 12. 24659-0 Pa. **$9.95**

HUMORESQUES AND OTHER WORKS FOR SOLO PIANO, Antonin Dvořák. Humoresques, Op. 101, complete, Silhouettes, Op. 8, Poetic Tone Pictures, Theme with Variations, Op. 36, 4 Slavonic Dances, more. 160pp. 9 × 12. 28355-0 Pa. **$9.95**

PIANO MUSIC, Louis M. Gottschalk. 26 pieces (including covers) by early 19th-century American genius. "Bamboula," "The Banjo," other Creole, Negro-based material, through elegant salon music. 301pp. 9¼ × 12. 21683-7 Pa. **$13.95**

SOUSA'S GREAT MARCHES IN PIANO TRANSCRIPTION, John Philip Sousa. Playing edition includes: "The Stars and Stripes Forever," "King Cotton," "Washington Post," much more. 24 illustrations. 111pp. 9 × 12. 23132-1 Pa. **$7.95**

COMPLETE PIANO RAGS, Scott Joplin. All 38 piano rags by the acknowledged master of the form, reprinted from the publisher's original editions complete with sheet music covers. Introduction by David A. Jasen. 208pp. 9 × 12. 25807-6 Pa. **$9.95**

RAGTIME REDISCOVERIES, selected by Trebor Jay Tichenor. 64 unusual rags demonstrate diversity of style, local tradition. Original sheet music. 320pp. 9 × 12. 23776-1 Pa. **$14.95**

RAGTIME RARITIES, edited by Trebor J. Tichenor. 63 tuneful, rediscovered piano rags by 51 composers (or teams). Does not duplicate selections in *Classic Piano Rags* (Dover, 20469-3). 305pp. 9 × 12. 23157-7 Pa. **$14.95**

CLASSIC PIANO RAGS, selected with an introduction by Rudi Blesh. Best ragtime music (1897–1922) by Scott Joplin, James Scott, Joseph F. Lamb, Tom Turpin, nine others. 364pp. 9 × 12. 20469-3 Pa. **$15.95**

RAGTIME GEMS: Original Sheet Music for 25 Ragtime Classics, edited by David A. Jasen. Includes original sheet music and covers for 25 rags, including three of Scott Joplin's finest: *Searchlight Rag, Rose Leaf Rag* and *Fig Leaf Rag*. 122pp. 9 × 12. 25248-5 Pa. **$8.95**

NOCTURNES AND BARCAROLLES FOR SOLO PIANO, Gabriel Fauré. 12 nocturnes and 12 barcarolles reprinted from authoritative French editions. 208pp. 9⅜ × 12¼. (Not available in France or Germany) 27955-3 Pa. **$12.95**

FAVORITE WALTZES, POLKAS AND OTHER DANCES FOR SOLO PIANO, Johann Strauss, Jr. Blue Danube, Tales from Vienna Woods, many other best-known waltzes and other dances. 160pp. 9 × 12. 27851-4 Pa. **$10.95**

SELECTED PIANO WORKS FOR FOUR HANDS, Franz Schubert. 24 separate pieces (16 most popular titles): Three Military Marches, Lebensstürme, Four Polonaises, Four Ländler, etc. Rehearsal numbers added. 273pp. 9 × 12. 23529-7 Pa. **$12.95**

Available from your music dealer or write for free Music Catalog to
Dover Publications, Inc., Dept. MUBI, 31 East 2nd Street, Mineola, N.Y. 11501.